"Out of the night that covers me,
Black as the pit from pole to pole,
I thank whatever gods may be
For my unconquerable soul.

In the fell clutch of circumstance
I have not winced nor cried aloud.
Under the bludgeonings of chance
My head is bloody, but unbowed.

Beyond this place of wrath and tears
Looms but the horror of the shade,
And yet the menace of the years
Finds, and shall find, me unafraid.

It matters not how strait the gate,
How charged with punishments the scroll,
I am the master of my fate:
I am the captain of my soul."

– William Ernest Henley, Invictus

VOLUNTARY
ADMISSION

VOLUNTARY ADMISSION

BY
ANTHONY BAYSS

Voluntary Admission

ISBN 978-0-9941728-0-8 (paperback)
ISBN 978-0-9941728-1-5 (ebook)

First edition, 2014
ISBN 978-0-9941728-0-8

DEDICATION

I would like to dedicate this book to all those suffering in silence. You must know you are not alone.

Millions of others have experienced the pain you are enduring and there is no stigma in asking for help to treat your agony.

You have to know depression and anxiety are illnesses, not weaknesses.

Family, friends, and a multitude of healthcare professionals are willing to listen to your needs and instigate the appropriate treatment. Being unable to speak to loved ones about your situation is not a stumbling block. I sought help from people I had never met before – so can you.

On seeking assistance you will not be judged by the questions you ask; rather you will be handled with dignity and respect by specialists who treat these illnesses daily.

There are always solutions to the problems on which you are fixated. All you need to do is offer those three words – "I need help."

TO MY FAMILY AND FRIENDS

The decision to write this book was motivated by your reaction to my hospitalization.

I experienced your unwavering encouragement from the moment you received that heart-stopping phone call.

Every day I am gifted with your love and support.

It was not until after I was discharged from the Psychiatric Emergency Care Centre that I began to understand how my suicide would have left you with much pain.

Your persistent inspiration for breaking my negative observations of life have provided me with a new beginning.

A start I am keen to not look back on.

CONTENTS

PREFACE

So how does a 34-year-old male, who is shy, depressed, and suicidal, handle life's issues?

At the time of writing this Preface I had just been discharged from a twelve-day voluntary visit to the Psychiatric Emergency Care Centre (PECC) at the Prince of Wales Hospital, Sydney.

If I had not walked into the emergency department of the hospital and asked for help almost two weeks earlier I am sure that the thoughts of suicide would have rapidly returned to finish me off.

The doctors and nurses started listening to my worries within minutes of me presenting to hospital. And not one of those who were involved in my care judged me for my illness.

Looking back on my decision to ask for help, I now realize reaching rock bottom was not a precarious position to be in. My life to date had not taken me to where I envisaged all my hard work would; however, in stepping back from suicide and seeking assistance I acknowledge my journey can now start again.

On leaving the hospital I was warned that the treatment for major depression and attempted suicide was not going to be a quick journey, or one of linear direction.

INTRODUCTION

I want to make it very clear that this book does not outline cures for depression and should not be read as a way to self-diagnose any mental illness.

This book is deliberately short so no one has an excuse for not reading the contents.

This book is primarily written for those who are living with an undiagnosed mental illness. You will learn how asking for help can truly save your life. More importantly you will be encouraged to seek answers from loved ones and professionals after you discover the incredible treatment I received while as an inpatient and also after my discharge from hospital.

Voluntary Admission is also a fantastic eye-opener for those in the community who have had no experience or exposure to someone with a mental illness. You will uncover the insidious and indiscriminate nature of major depression. My personal encounters with mental illness are chronicled so you can understand how quickly these types of illnesses can spiral out of control.

The World Health Organization (WHO) estimates

there are three hundred and fifty million people world-wide suffering from depression, but only fifty percent are receiving treatment. Moreover, one million people commit suicide every year and about twenty million people attempt to commit suicide every year.

I wish for teenagers, young adults and mature aged groups to discover how mental illness can touch anyone, at any time in their life, and how it can rapidly become an uncontrollable illness.

We can talk openly about sports injuries, having the flu, or even some of the major health battles like cancer. If we have a headache, are feeling stressed, or have a pain in the stomach, all of which are not necessarily visible, we still can volunteer our painful experiences to others.

However, those experiencing depression, anxiety and suicidal tendencies are less likely to offer details of this illness to family and friends.

I believe the eradication of the stigma associated with depression and anxiety can only start after society acknowledges that we are dealing with an illness, not a weakness.

I want this book to be left on the coffee table, on the kitchen bench, or around the office for all eyes to view. The reluctance to include depression or anxiety in an open conversation with family or friends has to be broken.

CHAPTER 1

The Downward Spiral

I had always seen myself as a self-sufficient person, someone who never asked for help and could always find a solution to a problem on my own. How wrong I was.

In the weeks leading up to my suicide attempt my thought processes can only be characterized as erratic. In my head there were no conceivable answers to my many problems. The issues I overly fixated upon included business venture problems, the multiple legal wranglings with different parties, that I did not enjoy my occupation, student loan debt, and my self-inflicted nonexistent social life. It seemed that everything I tried to fix these problems was only yanking those unrealistic expectations constructed over the years further from my reach. I was drowning.

Quitting my paid job in the hospitality industry was only a matter of time. I came to hate the job and the lack of career direction. Work paid the bills but only added to my misery. The only rewarding aspect was the people I met. I did form some strong friendships with work colleagues and customers; however, the work environment became untenable.

I did not meet my last day of work with joy or a sense of relief; rather I only redirected the churn of negative thoughts to the many other stresses I was dealing with.

As the days went by the negative thoughts about life began to spiral out of control.

The business venture was only amassing more brick walls, I had no new career direction and was physically exhausted from working ridiculous hours since leaving school.

Thoughts of finding a new job in the hospitality industry were persistent, as I needed to afford living expenses. I became physically sick before a couple of job interviews because I simply could not imagine working in an environment I loathed. I had become stuck.

This feeling was becoming more than just unsettling. Stress and anxiety became a daily battle, now immune to a lengthy walk or any forms of comfort confectionary.

I began to withdraw from the world that seemed to only be against me. I was sleeping much more during the day but my nightly absence of sleep increased. Five to ten times a night I would awaken, still trying to handle my many worries.

After about ten days of no paid work I began to retract from all social interactions I had left. I stopped using Facebook and delayed returning phone calls from even family and friends. Thoughts of hopelessness and not wanting to continue on with life began to gather pace in my mind.

My irritability and sense of worthlessness amplified every day. Withdrawing from all communication solved the daily experiences of heart palpitations when the phone rang or when emails were pushed through to my phone. I stopped answering the phone when family rang and constantly cancelled dinner or lunch plans with loved ones. I had no interest in engaging with anyone.

I spent many fleeting moments thinking about the worries I had amassed and created in my head. I was unable to concentrate on each issue and moved on to the next concern out of frustration for not being able solve any problems. My thoughts jumped from one stressful, worthless discomfort to the next, only exacerbating my feeling of hopelessness.

Days were reduced to sleeping, eating, and walking. I only left the house to try to hide my worries from Dad. A ten or fifteen kilometer walk was now a daily event. I was not interested in the passing scenery or the fresh air but rather the time spent pushing the block of complications through my head. The extra time spent outside during that winter even rewarded me with a suntan. Nothing positive came from this mental torment; it only pushed my state of mind towards a feeling of inescapable pain.

Breaking point came on Thursday 31st July when I knew the following week I would be unable to meet my share of the rent. The encircling unsolvable problems kept me awake all night and I set out early for another long, pointless walk. My continued heart palpitation whenever new emails came in or the mobile phone rang was a constant reminder of how even a little event would send my nerves off. Of course I avoided anyone's attempt to communicate with me.

The agonizing feeling of being stuck with no way out could only be compared with one previous experience.

In Year Nine at school, as part of our compulsory outdoor camping course, I had to take part in a caving exercise. At first I had no nerves about exploring cold, wet, pitch-black caves.

As I moved further through the caves the restricted spaces grew into mere narrow cracks. I had become wedged in a black hole with my plastic hard hat jammed between two muddy boulders. It was only as the unfamiliar space began to close in on me that my anxiety increased along with a feeling of helplessness. I can remember my stress levels drastically rising and severe panic set in until I slowly worked my way out of the tight spot.

My current situation felt the same, only exacerbated one hundred fold.

I must have walked around for four or five hours, with no specific route or destination planned. I can remember spending time at the cliffs at Clovelly Beach, and at the water's edge at Double Bay, but it was the heavy traffic on Darley Road that caught my attention.

The Suicide Attempt

It is extremely difficult to even think about what state of mind I was in when I attempted to step in front of the traffic coming down the hill. I would say that I was numb with pain.

I did not want to ponder my perceived failures anymore; I did not want to communicate with loved ones, friends, collegaues or customers anymore; and I was unable to imagine any positive way forward. I had given up.

What happened next can only be described as something I participated in with no reluctance. It also took place so quickly I had no ability to impede the dangerous action.

My irrational thinking allowed me to leave the footpath and begin to align with the large truck moving down the hill. I was drawn to the truck's path; however, the driver saw me crossing and applied the brakes.

My negativity kicked in: knowing my luck any direct hit would not kill me, just leave me severely injured, perhaps a quadriplegic, so I moved out of the way.

I can remember a sense of disappointment set in as I stepped back onto the footpath.

I had not planned to step in front of the truck; the situation presented itself and I was in no state of mind to stop the temptation. These actions were undertaken as if my body was no longer in control of itself. The speed at which these irrational steps took power over my body was alarming.

I continued my walk, and it was at least an hour later when it dawned on me that I was in no mental state to make rational decisions. I needed immediate professional help.

Regrouping my thoughts

After this failed attempt I ended up back down at Clovelly Beach. The weather was unusually warm for a winter's day so I moved from the bench seats in the sun to a more shaded area. I had no more strength to keep walking. The next couple of hours were spent hydrating from the nearby water bubblers and trying to rationalize the past couple of days.

I now knew my mental state had deteriorated and I now switched my thoughts to seeking help. The sky-high level of expectation I had generated for myself over the past eighteen years had now created another obstacle – there was no way I could talk to family or friends about my mental state. I was too embarrassed.

I headed towards Prince of Wales Hospital. I had been there the month before when Dad had a heart attack so I had a clear memory of how accommodating the emergency department staff were. As I set out, text messages came in from Dad. He was cooking dinner and it would be ready soon.

My destination was still set for the hospital, until more distractions arose. More text messages from Dad saying he had prepared dinner initiated a change in my course. Then by chance I ran into two family friends separately. I slipped on my wraparound sunglasses to hide the pain in my eyes. These two brief exchanges switched my mood back to a numb state. I arrived home for a meal to recharge my exhaustion and another a sleepless night.

I pondered approaching Dad in the morning to

ask for help; I even practiced the lines in my head, but was unable to convey my pain in a way he might understand. I finished breakfast, a couple cups of coffee. and left to complete my plan.

Before leaving the house I deliberately left my computer on, with all email accounts open on the screen so they could be accessed. I wrote down all my logins and passwords for bank accounts and from other critical suppliers on spare pieces of paper and set them out on my computer desk. I made sure I left my house keys at home to force me not to change my mind. I then left the house determined to remedy my mental state.

"I Need Help"

To build up my courage to present myself to hospital I set out on a walk for about an hour. After leaving Centennial Park I walked past The University of New South Wales and through Kingsford. I found Barker Street and the entrance to the hospital. Following one last lap of the surrounding streets I turned in the direction my depression necessitated.

I had reached the emergency department of the Prince of Wales Hospital and knew that help would be found within these walls.

The reception acknowledged my three words, "I need help," and after some paperwork I was ushered into the adjacent Triage Room. Within seconds I had begun to outline the previous 24 hours and the nurse, with a trainee on-looking, was making notes on her computer. A plastic hospital ID was placed on my right wrist and I was immediately taken through to where all the action was taking place.

Moving into the main emergency room, where all the doctors and nurses were attending patients, removed my worries. My state of mind was now more of a numb feeling. I had made the right decision but was still apprehensive about the coming hours and days.

Admitting myself into hospital was clearly a function of not being able to deal with the stigma of depression. I found it too uncomfortable to speak to family or friends. I thought the best approach was for me to seek help from a stranger who was a health professional. I felt they would not judge me. I was correct.

Over the next couple of hours I was seen multiple times by the same nurse. She did everything possible to ensure my wait was comfortable. The standard procedures were also undertaken – they checked my blood pressure, temperature, drew some blood, arranged for my family members to be notified of where I was – and they continued to reassure me the mental health team would do everything to address my situation.

I requested not to speak to my family members, who had dropped everything and rushed to the hospital upon receiving that phone call. The immediate pain this call must have caused them I could only imagine; however, I was in no state to communicate my thoughts to them.

The next interaction was with a psychiatrist and his trainee. This was my first contact with such a professional and I simply answered all his questions and he clearly explained that immediate medical assistance would be provided. The doctor's tone and concise outline of the events to follow made me realize I had finally made the correct decision to present myself at hospital.

CHAPTER 2

Who am I

Following my admission into hospital I was asked background information by many different psychiatrists. My answers to their questions can be found in this small brief about myself:

I am 34 years old. I was born in Sydney and grew up in the same city. My parents are true working class; they have operated cafes and restaurants for as long as I can remember, working either six or seven days a week. I have two brothers: one older and one younger.

We were afforded a fortunate education at a private Sydney school, but our family lives were as grounded as any other working class family. While I was growing up our family unit was very close. We had a structured family life where daily family meals together were a norm.

I see myself as very shy, moral, and a loyal person who makes only calculated decisions. I care about everything I undertake and find myself worrying and stressing about everything. I hardly drink, never take drugs and have never smoked. My shyness manifests itself in my lack of confidence I have when partaking in most events.

After completing high school I continued my education at the University of New South Wales where I studied a Bachelor of Arts degree.

The purpose of detailing my character is to point out how even someone like myself, who is well educated, comes from a loving family, and is physically fit, can be struck down with major depression. Mental illness does not discriminate.

Only Experiencing the Best

My school years from kindergarten through to Year Twelve were spent at an exclusive private boys school in Sydney, where I perceived monetary privilege to be the foundation for a happy life. This privilege was rooted in having the opportunity to go to a private school, where the exposure to wealth and high society became a daily occurrence.

I wholeheartedly thank my parents for the many years they struggled to pay the private school fees for their three sons, but on reflection, my experiences at school were void of the real world daily problems.

My earliest memories go back to playing in the sand pit, and it is from those early moments that I can begin to construct the story for the direction I thought my life would take.

Throughout school I felt that I did not really fit in. By fitting in, I mean with the class of society the majority of the students came from. I also received passing shots about my chubbiness, something that was consistently annoying.

My parents were very much working class. They were hard working people who devoted twenty years of their lives to ensure their three children had the best education possible. Yes they did an amazing job.

The most prominent reminder of this social class difference was the inability to attend overseas trips organized each year – they were simply outside my parents' budget. I was not overly disappointed about missing out, but the fact that it was not even an option for me was a nagging reminder of how wealth introduces one to more privileges.

Today my best friends do come from school; however, I was somehow able to mix in circles with friends who had similar socioeconomic back-grounds to me. I saw those friends as people I could. relate to.

Even the Views Were Amazing

I can remember on almost every New Years Eve during my teens we were able to find the best views for the fireworks from the school grounds.

These uninterrupted picture postcard views of the Sydney Harbour Bridge I took for granted every single day. I did not realize this until the last couple of years of school, when I had more study time, but which was not spent studying but taking in the amazing scenery I was previously too young to appreciate. Sydney houses that had these views could easily command millions on the housing market.

Throughout the corridors of the school's administration building there were donation boards, outlining those individuals or families who had previously given money for the future development of the school's facilities. I can remember thinking to myself that one day I will be able to proudly see my name embossed on the dark stained board, as it was a symbol of success.

The school grounds were always immaculately presented with sweeping grand driveways, newly building constructions underway, and the ever-increasing line of new luxury cars waiting in the afternoon pickup traffic jam. The Hollywood-like lifestyle did not end when school finished on Fridays.

Weekend sport was another event that took me up to some of the most wealthy suburbs of the Upper Northshore of Sydney. The sporting grounds of the other schools we played at matched the conditions of the school I attended. Arriving at these leafy suburbs was not short of a journey in itself. The suburbs were lined with grand mansions and the teams we played against were filled with students of the same pedigree.

As I progressed through the school years, the extent of how wealth opened up doors and presented many more opportunities in life became more apparent.

Throughout my years at school there were weekend birthday parties for schoolmates to attend. These events provided me more affirmation that my classmates' lifestyles were something to aspire to. I can remember attending many waterfront houses, riding in all types of luxury cars, and the hosts' family names read like a who's who of society and the captains of industry.

The many extra school holidays private schools are gifted with meant the first couple of days of each new term were a lesson in what I had missed out on. Stories of who went to which countries to experience the latest in luxury holidaying became an agonizing ritual each and every new school term. I have still not been overseas yet; I guess I have more to look forward to than them!

Being a Prefect in the school cafeteria gave me even more examples of how my schooling environment was so far from social reality. So many students would open their wallets to pay for a $1 cookie, but all they had in their possession would be a wad of fifty-dollar notes. How do young people begin to understand the value of money if this is their daily norm?

It seemed there was a million ways money could buy happiness.

I think the envy that grew inside me as the years progressed turned into a desire to have what I thought I was missing out on. It is without doubt that I wish every person who works hard to be able to enjoy the spoils, and I am sure a vast majority of those families who sent their children to the school were simply acting on this pleasure. Put simply, I now wanted to work hard to achieve the same.

Studying Hard

I was never a gifted student. I needed to work to earn good academic marks. I always felt the need to perform well in exams and to behave in class, and not abuse the privilege of good education my parents worked so hard to afford. I actually found it disturbing how some students behaved so disgracefully towards teachers, given the cost of the education for which their parents were outlaying.

From early on my areas of interest were economics, commence, and subjects that I could see to be of relevance in real life. By the time I was in Year Eight or Nine it was clear to me that being around financially privileged people had shaped my thoughts on what I wanted to do or become later in life. Rich and successful were the images I carried around for the remainder of my schooling years. My interests in business studies, economics, and computers grew as I observed that like-minded students enrolled in these subjects all the way up to Year Twelve.

I can remember I achieved well in a couple assignments that required us to theoretically establish a business. The marks I received from these types of assessments gave me confidence that I could simply repeat the practice in real life and that the outcomes would be wealth and success.

The countless number of exams, assignments, and presentations from Year Ten until the end of Year Twelve was the beginning of a level of stress and anxiety that I can clearly evoke. The desire to perform well in these assessments did not stop until the middle of November 1997 when my last exam had finished. I can remember being physically and mentally rundown from this process.

The growing level of homework kept me up late at night and consumed my weekends. I considered myself a conscientious student, willing to work hard to ensure I maintained an above average academic standing. However, the daily stress of school now turned into a nightly stress of ensuring I completed all my homework. My parents had a strict no television on weekdays policy. I will probably enact the same policy when I have children; however, I am certain this decision interfered with my heightened stress and anxiety over school work.

The hard work required to maintain acceptable academic results, usually through countless hours of rote-learning, showed me that preferred results could be achieved. My mother pulled me aside at the end of Year Ten and said that I would need to be self-motivated to achieve my goals. She was right; I needed to find a set of goals to work towards.

My parents did not force me into studying any particular subjects; they supported me with whatever informed decisions I made. What I did not know was that my entire experience at school until this time had helped shape what I was going to spend the next eighteen years of my life wrongfully chasing: greater financial wealth to achieve greater happiness.

To provide support to students with their potential career choices, the school employed a full-time careers adviser. I found the hours spent with this person to be of no help what so ever. The results from all the questionnaires I filled in, with the purpose of narrowing the optimum alternatives for my future career path, were discouraging. Their computer modeling concluded that I should be a park ranger!

In addition, career evenings were arranged each year where ex students and parents would speak about their profession to give pupils a better insight into different career paths. The idea of being able to come back to school and preach my successful profession to future students sat well with my growing expectations of myself. But by the time I got to Year 12 I still had no idea which profession I wanted to pursue; all I knew was that I wanted to have a big house and live the lifestyle I would soon be privileged to experience.

I can recall the many weekend sporting events where I would be either standing on the sideline of the field or crowded around the food stalls after the games. I would overhear the parents discuss their colorful lifestyles. The chatter jumped from where the next holiday would be, to what social events would be occurring that night, or to where they were travelling next. Frequent mentions of weekend visits to hobby farms or beach houses up the coast were backed up by their cars being fully stocked for the upcoming trip.

It was only years later that I pieced together the absurd effects my experience of attending a private school had on my perception of what matters in life.

The education itself was fantastic. The teachers were amazing, and I only have good things to say about my parents who toiled to ensure their children had the best education. There is no doubt that exposure to this level of privilege while my family was from a working class society acted as a trampoline, exacerbating the gap between how far and fast I would fall back to reality later in life.

CHAPTER 3

PECC Day 1 – Friday

It was not an uncomfortable amount of time before I was moved into a specialist department – the Psychiatric Emergency Care Centre (PECC).

On first observation I noticed how small and quiet it was. The center consisted of a large open common room with a kitchenette, dining table, lounge and a couple of televisions. Adjacent to this was a large staff office divided by large enclosed windows. Straight ahead were four unobtrusive private rooms and two toilet facilities. A little courtyard and a two consultation rooms were also attached. There was even an internal laundry.

Nursing staff walked me through all the paperwork that needed to be completed before showing me to my private room. I was informed that I could contact family members at any time and they could also phone me.

I found my way into the hospital bed and fell

into a four- or five-hour sleep. My anxiety levels were still of a concern but I now knew my actions had instigated that professional help my mental state was crying out for.

A nursing staff woke me up for a 5pm dinner. I can honestly not remember what the meal entailed, but I ate it with no contest. Dessert and coffee was also served.

I received three phone calls before bed. My older brother, then my dad and then my mother all rang to open up a dialogue. I instructed the nurse to decline all three. I simply was in no state to talk to the people who meant the most to me. I still had a sense of embarrassment.

I returned to my bed for more much-needed sleep.

About an hour later the same nurse returned to start me on a dose of antidepressants. The night can be described as interrupted sleep, with many thoughts still swirling through my head.

PECC Day 2 – Saturday

Throughout the night I had noticed nurses moving down the corridor; it seemed to be methodical all night long.

I was woken with a polite knock at the door,

announcing that breakfast was ready. It must have been around 8am. No meals could be unconsumed in the bedrooms so all patients were forced to congregate in the common room. The dining table was large enough for four patients.

Weetabix, toast, orange juice, and coffee. This was the start of a twelve day stay during which I would be well fed. I was unable to find the toaster; rather I had to hand over the two pieces of white bread to the nurse who returned to her office to toast my bread for me. She reappeared a couple of minutes later with my two slices of toast ready for me to butter. There were little indications like this that I overlooked and it was not for a couple of days that I pieced together these little observations.

I had received another phone message from my brother to inform me that he and my dad would be in to visit in a couple of hours.

My plan to return to bed was thwarted by the first daily psychiatrist consultation. I was whisked off into a consultation room that I am sure I visited the day before, this time with a different psychiatrist and trainee staff member.

I presented a repeat of my brief life history and another overview of what had occurred in the previous 24 hours. This story of events was still extremely painful and raw. The doctor outlined her preliminary diagnosis of major depression and also clearly structured the events that would occur from here. The one subject that would be repeated throughout my stay in PECC was my perception of how safe I felt and if my thoughts ever returned to those agonizing moments of suicide.

This question was followed by a self-rating of my mood out of ten, zero being the lowest mood and ten being the highest/good mood. As my days in the unit progressed this number moved up to peak at five; obviously it started out at zero.

I returned to my bed to try again to fall asleep.

The distant noise that quickly turned into the noticeable voices of my dad and older brother interrupted my sleep and made me realize that it was now time to face my family with my previously well-hidden illness. The next hour was going to be necessary, but immensely difficult for all three of us.

I would not be telling the truth if I did not mention the uncontrollable tears that were accompanying my confession, as I was unable to control my emotions in front of my family members. The ease at which my feeling flowed out once I started was a surprise even to me.

My family members responded with compassion and support. They did not judge me in any way and continued to reassure me that the problems I perceived to be weighing me down could be resolved.

My brother's and Dad's rational words began to break down my irrational view my life and what the future held for me. They continued to make very clear that my decision to simply ask for help was the greatest choice I could have made.

I asked my older brother to contact my younger brother, who was overseas on holidays, and let him know he should not worry about my hospitalization, and to enjoy the rest of this trip.

My older brother accepted my request to help sort through my financial situation. Even his acceptance gave me a sense of relief that someone with a sound mind was willing to help address my issues.

My family's reaction to my situation showed me how I should react with other family or friends if they ever found themselves in my position.

Confronting my family members with my problems should have occurred earlier, an enormous regret I can now acknowledge.

I said goodbye to my brother and Dad as lunch was being wheeled into the room. Their visit had distracted me from my low mood and I was now trying to enforce their instruction: "Do not worry about anything, there is always a way forward. Your problems are fixable."

In between lunch and dinner my attempt to get

some sleep was interrupted by another phone call from my mother. I could not find the courage to even speak to her; I was afraid of speaking or seeing her while I was in this state.

I had no motivation to try to start a conversation with the other three patients hanging out in the common room watching television. I needed to address my exhaustion.

PECC Day 3 – Sunday

My light sleep was interrupted by the methodic half-hour pacing of the nightshift nursing staff. After catching them multiple times peeking into my room through the window, it finally dawned on me. I had put the pieces together.

As part of the check-in processes, I had handed over all my belongings, even my belt. This unit was small and the staff-to-patient ratio was high. Their rules were discrete: no metal cutlery, not being able to use the toaster, no phones, no internet access, and constant observation – the gravity of the situation was clear. I was on suicide watch.

After cereal, toast, and a couple of coffees, my recurrent sleep was interjected by the daily psychiatrist consultation.

A different doctor on duty asked me to repeat my explanation of the events leading up my voluntary admission into hospital. These consultations were always constructive; they were necessary to evaluate my mood and to determine how my treatment should progress. My stress and anxiety had subsided, and my mood may have shifted up a notch, but little events triggered my nerves.

The hospital was aware of my private health insurance coverage as I mentioned this on my admission form. PECC advised that a private hospital would provide a more quiet environment for the long treatment time ahead. Plans were in place to arrange for a transfer into an already identified facility.

I rejected another phone call from Mum. I left a message for her, promising to return her four phone calls by the end of the day.

After eating a hot roast chicken and steamed vegetable lunch, Dad came in again for a visit.

I noticed he was stressed about seeing me in this situation. He did his best to reassure me that my wrongfully constructed views of my current financial situation and career prospects were solvable. My anxiety was lower than the day before but I knew it would be some time before I caught up on sleep.

Dad had brought me clothes, toiletries, and biscuits. We spoke for about half an hour before I lost interest in the conversation. I excused myself and headed off for another sleep.

Dinner was served like clockwork and I was able to work my way through the sizable portion, side of bread, chocolate pudding and after meal coffee.

I kept my promise and asked the nurse if I could make a phone call.

The conversation with Mum was easier than the one I had with my brother and Dad a couple days earlier. I had learnt from my previous talk with my family they were only there to support my recovery. My preconception that I would be judged or feel embarrassed by explaining my situation to family was wrong.

CHAPTER 4

From One Utopia to Another

I can clearly remember the very last school function where the whole school farewelled each student individually and we symbolically walked out of the large gymnasium. On leaving the building I can recall turning around and looking back at the crowd inside and thinking to myself, "Well that's it, what now?"

For me school was a bubble, a utopian life that had ended, and I had not prepared for the real world. Realizing the financial struggles my parents endured in sending my two brothers and me to one of the best private schools the country had to offer, there was a huge level of expectation I placed on myself.

This sense of expectation was growing and was always in the back of my mind from the beginning of Year Eleven. I remember selecting the subjects I wanted to do for the last two years of school. I had formed the view that I owed it to my parents, friends and to the school society to create a life for myself that matched the lifestyle I was immersed in while at school. Thus, I had to have an immaculately landscaped house, luxury cars and a successful business. I had created the opinion that my happiness was directly dependent on fitting in with this high society I had just left.

No Time to Unwind

As soon as the exam period ended I noticed I could not turn my mind off. I had stressful thoughts turning over in my head that would not stop. I could not relax. The stressful thoughts were about the pending exams results and trying to determine what career path to take, so the notion of going on a holiday to celebrate the end of school was not an option for me. I started work the next day.

Working was not new to me; I had spent many holidays helping out in my parents' cafes and restaurants. I could relate to working hard; it mirrored my efforts of years of rote learning for exams – hard work seemed to have a similar reward. I did not mind the early mornings or the long hours, as it kept my mind distracted. At that stage, my shyness kept me from wanting to interact with the public, so cooking and prepping in the kitchen was a far as I could venture.

Over the following weeks, I began to hear the stories about my friends' wild holidays and other events that occurred post-exams.

The Results –
The Disappointment Starts

My next big stressful event was waiting for the Year Twelve exam results. For a Year Twelve student (and their family), that final mark out of 100 is the make or break moment for the next step in their life. I was planning to do a degree in Commerce as I thought this tertiary education was required to establish a business empire.

Over the following days, I began to learn what everyone in my year achieved and how they would move forward into university. My plans were stunted by a mark I had to recheck a second time from the papers I had thrown across the room in disgust. A score of 85.7 was not a result reflecting the hard work I had put in, and it sure was not enough to enter any of my top five universities I had identified months ago while sitting in the career adviser's office. Perhaps I should have selected that park ranger occupation!

I can remember the following month or two was spent working, drinking and pondering how to meet my career expectations with no relevant university placing selected. This uncertainty and unease about how I was going to move forward added to the general stress I already carried .

I made a last minute decision to enroll in a BA degree at the University of New South Wales, with the intent to switch to a more relevant degree after the end of my first year. I still did not know the exact profession I wanted to pursue; all I knew was that I wished to have a life for myself and my future family that emulated my schoolmates' lifestyles. Not having an exact plan to move forward caused me much anxiety and worry. I knew this tension was unwarranted; I should have been enjoying this time.

CHAPTER 5

PECC Day 4 – Monday

Following the routine breakfast and two coffees I was happily informed Dad was coming back for another visit. Some existing patients were discharged that morning so there were lots of people busy finishing lots of paperwork.

Dad arrived with a big smile of his face. He came bearing good news. I got changed into fresh clothes, and after some more paperwork I was allowed outside on a one-hour escorted leave.

I did not have the energy to walk too far so we found a seat at the main hospital café about a two-minute walk away. I found this environment to be very loud and confronting, such a juxtaposition from the past four days. I wanted to return to PECC.

My conversation with Dad wavered from my feelings, the quality of the food I was eating, to how the other family members were, and who else had been informed of my hospitalization.

I was already concerned about how others would perceive my reason for being here.

Dad reassured me that only immediate family knew of my illness and that no one else would be told without my consent. My mind was many steps ahead; I was already envisioning the very arduous conversations the future would present. At some point in time, I would have to explain my illness and absence to good friends and other family members. I was already stressing and rehearsing those lines.

After about 30 minutes I had lost interest in talking about anything. Dad returned me to PECC where a psychiatrist and her trainee intercepted my plan of a short sleep for a consultation.

On the morning of the previous Friday, I had decided that it was time to ask for help. This involved being open about my thoughts, my past, and how my mood was tracking. That day I had hidden something from my Dad: that the suicidal thoughts had returned.

I understood being unguarded about my mental state was paramount in obtaining the correct treatment. I told the psychiatrist that my suicidal thoughts had raised their ugly heads again. This was a difficult confession.

The psychiatrist responded by starting me on medication in an attempt to eradicate those thoughts.

I returned to the common room, but became frustrated with my inability to concentrate on simple tasks like reading or watching television.

My concentration was going to be tested; I had discovered a five hundred piece jigsaw puzzle of a black and white 1920's city landscape. I made myself another coffee and settled into the lounge chair for a mental workout.

I was interrupted by the dinner trolley being wheeled into the common room. Roast pork and steamed vegetables were served in the customary sealable, disposable plastic plate. I finished everything served to me, including dessert and a glass of orange juice.

For a couple of hours leading up to bedtime I alternated between finding all the edge pieces of the puzzle and watching interrupted segments of whatever was showing on television. My nightly medication now included two pills.

PECC Day 5 – Tuesday

I slept straight through the noise generated by the predictable corridor walks of the nightly nursing staff. Getting a full nine hours sleep left my head foggy. My sleep was only interrupted by an abrupt knock on the door, followed by the nurse telling me that breakfast had been waiting for me for some time. I hated being late so I quickly leapt out of bed. My inability to be on time was evidence the anti-psychotic drugs were taking effect.

Today was to bring many occurrences.

PECC had started the arrangements for my transfer to a private hospital a couple of suburbs away. I wholeheartedly appreciated the efforts every doctor and nurse had done for me; however, I was looking forward to a facility my monthly private health insurance should have afforded me.

It was not to be.

The private hospital had booked my transfer for the next day and they were on the phone to PECC to confirm all my details. Apparently private hospital cover does not necessarily mean full coverage. Over the phone I was quoted a $480 per day gap charge. My heart sank and my anger brewed.

I had no money to pay these daily charges, and I quickly realized this option would have meant money poorly spent anyway. I had now experienced my fifth day of exceptional healthcare, so why should I pay a third party to try to replicate what I was currently receiving?. I was truly privileged to live in a country where the public healthcare system was second to none.

The nurses in PECC were very quick to let me know that I could stay there until a bed in the general psychiatric ward became free. My nerves were temporarily settled.

A trainee doctor pulled me aside to ask what felt like a hundred questions in preparation for the upcoming MRI of my brain. There were lots of questions to ensure I had no metal objects on my person during the scan. I had previously had an MRI on my left knee, so I understood the process. I was more concerned about the claustrophobic nature of the procedure.

The hot lunch delivery was delayed by my daily psychiatrist consultation. My disappointment in not being able to afford the transfer to a private hospital escalated when the consulting doctor cautioned me about the general ward. He said that the illnesses other patients were being treated for would be confronting to me.

My mind quickly escaped to movies and television shows that depicted the norm in a psychiatric hospital.

I was reassured that the stereotypes on television did not represent reality. The doctor clarified that the general ward was confronting but safe. I ended the meeting by confessing my mood was probably at about a four out of ten.

My afternoon visitor was not who I expected. A

nurse arrived to take more blood. Besides the mosquito-like sting of the needle I had no issue with this task, as long as I did not watch the blood flowing from my arm.

The rest of the day was occupied with eating lunch, dinner, and getting excessive sleep – all side effects of the extra medication.

After dinner, the nurses proceeded with their routine of dispensing medication and checking blood pressure, temperature, and oxygen in the blood.

One of the many aspects of PECC life I found to be very comforting was how the nurses spent their breaks. Mostly they spent their time in the common room with the patients, talking about daily events or any topic that came to hand. This extra interaction demonstrates how the nursing staff truly have a passion for their work.

PECC Day 6 – Wednesday

Like clockwork, the nurse who notified me that breakfast had arrived ended my drug-assisted sleep.

The very small and quiet nature of the PECC meant that I was somewhat secluded from the rest of the world. I had to constantly ask nurses what day of the week it was.

Over the past couple of days I had felt the need to eat much more than normal. I quickly made my way through a couple of Weetabixs, two slices of raisin toast, a coffee, and an orange juice.

I got all the way through breakfast before I realized what the medication was doing. My thoughts were not racing, my mind was not forming my default negative conclusions. Perhaps my mood had moved up a notch to five out of ten.

After breakfast, I continued my attempt at the large puzzle started the day before. I found this exercise relaxing; it definitively withdrew me from all the other places my mind could drift off to.

By mid-morning PECC had received a new patient and also accommodated some family and friends of current patients who had come to visit their loved ones.

The PECC unit was not only a facilitator of healthcare services. The nurses introduced me to a social worker, whose job was to advise me on whether I was entitled to any government assistance.

I found this an extremely sensitive topic as in the past I had never asked for any help. In fact, I wrongly believed that accepting government assistance was a symbol of my failure.

Dad sat in on the meeting with the social worker as my ability to absorb details on any subject at this time was handicapped. The social worker arranged for a phone interview with the Department of Human Services for the following Monday.

On the day of my MRI brain scan, I was escorted through the labyrinth of hospital corridors by one of the PECC nurses. I dreaded the following twenty minutes, as the confined space reminded me of that caving event so many years ago.

Again I was asked if I had any metal objects on or in my body before being directed to the MRI machine. The time in the machine was uncomfortable, but the noise of the machine was more confronting than the confined space.

After lunch, I had my daily psychiatrist consultation. I aired my grievances about my need to accept government benefits and how it affected my mood. The doctor explained there was an unspecified waiting period before I could be moved down to the general psychiatric ward. At the time, my location was of no concern to me because I was more anxious about the exact time the anti-depressants would take effect.

Before dinner, I was able to catch a couple of hours sleep. Both my older brother and mother called to see how I was feeling and to reassure me my problems were solvable.

I began to realize I would have to spend less time worrying about so many different issues. My time in

PECC helped me establish this vital, newly learnt habit.

Before bed, I returned to my puzzle and I was finally able to fill the last remaining empty spaces. Along with my daily medication, the night nurse provided me with detailed information on drugs I was taking. Being unable to concentrate, I skipped through the pages, only stopping on the section listing the known side effects.

CHAPTER 6

University and Utopia

I spent three years at university moving from subject to subject, trying to find an area of interest that motivated me. I treated every subject like I did my schoolwork; I cared about performing well and constantly placed pressure on myself to accomplish above average marks. Subjects varied from politics, history, media, law, business, economics, ethics, science and technology, sociology, and even education studies. For the first couple of years I struggled to fit into university life because I was unable to identify a direction that would allow me to ease the expectations I had created during my school years.

This frustration exacerbated as my time at university crept towards graduation. Discovering how my previous schoolmates and university colleagues had secured cadetships, were finalizing a specialized degree, or were even establishing their own businesses, all heightened my unease about how I was going to meet my own expectations.

While studying five days a week and partying a couple of nights a week, I also worked weekends at my parents' café. As the years progressed, I began pushing myself out of the kitchen operations and moved onto the floor. I wanted to face my shyness head-on. Slowly I began to interact more comfortably with customers, but to this day I still have an underlying dread for meeting and talking to the general public.

I contemplated dropping out of the degree several times but I did not want to give the perception that I had failed. I never discussed this stigma with anyone; I just imagined that others would form this view. I can remember considering a career in areas that were not held by anyone I knew – areas like criminology, the army, police force, or social work. These types of occupations drew me in as having a job that involved helping others in need would reflect my true character. Opposing these interests would turn out to be a monumental mistake, but it was a huge learning curve in what really matters in life.

Studying and working more hours, I began to notice I was losing weight. I could still eat whatever I liked but the gradual reduction was commented on by friends and family. How things had changed – as a kid I was bullied for the chubbiness. Perhaps I was stressing the weight away.

On recollection, I think I began to become complacent about the real world. At the time, the bills were getting paid, but I was clearly not planning for the future I wanted to lead. Maybe I did not want to grow up.

The real test for what type of person I am was reflected in the answer to one question. By the time I had reached university I had been asked many times what I would do if I won a million dollars. My true answer was I would enjoy giving it away. This response was in direct conflict with my ambitions because they had to live up to my internal expectations. I pushed the real answer to the back of my mind.

I reassured myself regarding my decision to bury my true career interests by addressing my financial situation. Hospitality is not a well-paid occupation and along with the mistreatment by customers, I also began to dislike the work. I knew I was helping my parents with their business but I began to find the work boring, with no real room for career advancement.

Upon reaching the final year of my degree, I grew more anxious about how I would find a career path within the coming months. I still had no direction, but the many twenty-first birthday parties I attended distracted me throughout the entire year.

As the final session of university came around, I became immersed in subjects that involved technology, history and business. This subject combination made me contemplate how my misguided goals could be realized. Finishing university was not celebrated or mourned; I quietly just stepped off campus.

Looking back on it now, going to university was a waste of my time. My attendance did nothing to guide me toward a particular career. Perhaps I needed to try different occupations to determine a career path best for me.

The subjects I had studied only created a list of what I did not want to do or was not interested in pursuing. I came out of university a little more learned about a variety of topics but still lost about my life's direction. I was eerily retreading footsteps I previously walked leaving the high school gymnasium just three years earlier.

Business is not for Me

The time between leaving university until the my suicide attempt can only be described as fourteen years of non-stop tension. I see this period of my life as a lesson learned, an experience in what happens when you do not follow what is most important in life. Those reading my story can judge if I am to blame for my position; I have learnt if you do not plan for a work–life balance the alternative can be life threatening.

For these fourteen years, my paid work was spent in cafes and restaurants owned by my parents or other business owners. Soon after finishing university, I established a side business with my family, we invented a safety product for the café industry, I believed this business idea would address my lifestyle ambitions.

I used the money earned from working the hospitality jobs, usually six days a week, to pay for the research and development costs associated with our other business. I did not allow for holiday, social or relaxation time as I was 100 percent driven to making our business venture work. Yes, I had placed all my eggs in one basket.

Working for my parents in their cafes and restaurants was not easy work, but the choice to stay employed in this environment was my decision. The very early morning starts were not too bad but it did prevent me from having late nights out. Hospitality work can be stressful on its own, but with family involved there are situations where the pressures can be overwhelming.

My parents divorced while they still ran a café together in the city. Looking back, the work environment was painful and I should have removed myself from the job. My loyalty to consider both sides of the situation made me feel obliged to stay and help out. The lesson learnt from this is that hard work and doing "the right thing" can sometimes be a kick in the backside.

And Life Sailed on by

I began to experience the negative effects of my delusional expectations. I became more withdrawn from my job, mostly working on autopilot. I only viewed the job as a means of paying for the lifestyle I dreamed of. I often could not attend birthday parties, weddings or other important friends' events because I was dedicated to earning funds to drive my business. Even Saturday nights were off limits for relaxation; I stayed at home to saving money or addressing the thousand things going on in my head to bring our invention to market.

Not being able to attend a good friend's wedding in Melbourne was a clue something was wrong. As the costs of doing business increased, my social life came to a halt. I had become a lifeless robot.

If life is about experiencing different things, then I was not living any form of an existence. Another example of my one-track mind lifestyle was my blank passport. I have lost count how many times friends returned from overseas recounting their journeys. My friends have visited all continents, while my international travel plans never went beyond, "Okay, I will do that next year."

It is amazing how I just kept on going, pushing aside my issues to try to fulfill the expectations that, after all these years, I had still convinced myself I had to bring to fruition. I was able to endure my parents' divorce, the passing of my last grandparent, the deaths of a couple of friends from shocking accidents, a few health scares, Dad's heart attack, my parents losing their retirement fund, and my strained relationships with my mum and other family members. As each of these events occurred, they seemed to numb me, to prepare me for the next episode that was on course to hit me. I spent no time trying to deconstruct the individual incidents; I simply focused on working 70 to 80 hours per week.

I can remember working a couple of Christmas Days, New Year's Eves and even New Year's Days. Working around this time of the year always made me jealous of those who are not employed in the retail or hospitality industries. All my friends seemed to be winding down and taking holidays, while I was working the hardest weeks of the year. I was always missing key parties and celebrations due to my work commitments.

In the past eighteen years, I have treated myself to two holidays: one to Hamilton Island to sit by the pool in the sun; and the other in Melbourne to catch up with friends. These two holidays were only about one week each, far too short to even begin to unwind. However, they were not real holidays. I still fielded phone calls from work and even checked emails while having drinks in the hotel bars. I could not escape thoughts relating to business while away, so my stress levels were not dented at all by this time away from home.

CHAPTER 7

PECC Day 7 – Thursday

Sleep was regularly disturbed by my tendency to worry about whatever I was focused on at the time. Currently it was my growing concern about moving to the general ward. If the psychiatrist had warned me about the confronting nature of many of the patients it must be something worth teasing my mind over.

With this raised anxiety, I worked my way through breakfast and finished with the customary coffee. I found myself back in the seat that accommodated my puzzle solving. Without realizing I had already started a new jigsaw puzzle to distract me from my many worries.

Following my morning medication, I spent the following hours alternating between testing my concentration on the puzzle, to trying to watch television. My restlessness was symptomatic of my illness.

I was soon again distracted, this time by a surprise visit from Mum. We decided to give the other patients in the common room some privacy by moving out into the small un-shaded courtyard. Multiple boxes of chocolates and a hug gave me a short spike in my mood.

The support I had received from my family members, the nursing staff and the doctors continued to be extremely comforting. It made me grasp how serious my mental illness had become and how close the downward spiral was to ending my life. I truly began to understand how simply asking for help altered the direction in my life.

We must have talked for about an hour, with Mum sharing the well wishes for a speedy recovery from the extended family. I told Mum about the unknown timeframe for my transfer to the general ward. She told me not to worry about what had not happened yet or about the environment in which I would be treated.

As we began to run out of things to talk about, lunch was wheeled into the common room.

I spent the rest of the day alternating between sleeping and eating. I was mindful that I needed to allow the antidepressants much more time to start working. To some extent, the excessive sleep kept my mind from allowing any negative thoughts to percolate out of control.

After dinner I was informed that the demand

for beds in the general psychiatric ward outstripped supply, thus I would not be moved before Monday. I began to think there must be patients with much worse mental illnesses than my depression. Perhaps I would be discharged straight from the PECC unit?

By bed time I had to find another meal as my appetite was growing. That jigsaw puzzle preoccupied my concentration before I gave up fighting the side effects of the sleeping pills.

PECC Day 8 – Friday

I had now been in PECC for seven days. The improvement in my mood had peaked to a rating of about five out of ten.

The repetition of three meals, constant conversations with medical staff and nurses, and copious hours of sleep every day had helped stabilize my condition. I therefore was able to get unescorted leave for one hour.

I decided to go for a brief walk through the grounds of the adjacent University of New South Wales. Being an alumnus of this school, I was familiar with the basic layout but the construction of many new buildings had disorientated my bearings.

The noise of the traffic and of so many people

moving between classes was confronting after the isolation of being in PECC for a week. As I ventured through the university campus, the I became more unsettled.

I noticed students quietly sitting in groups on the library lawn, and others enjoying the sunny winter day throwing a rugby ball around. All the cafes on campus were full, with café staff busy recharging the students' minds before the next classes.

My hour of unescorted leave was cut short. I could not tolerate noise after what I had become accustomed to over the previous week. I left the university campus realizing I was not ready for any direct integration back into society.

By the time I had returned to PECC, one patient had been discharged and other had been admitted. I began to ponder the likelihood of being discharged while my current mood levels were not increasing at a rate I had anticipated.

Before and after lunch I continued with the jigsaw puzzle, trying to force my mind into a higher level of concentration. I was eventually distracted by the need for more sleep.

My daily consultation with the psychiatrist took place just before dinner. I described the unease I felt during the unescorted walk and explained that my days were now mostly filled with sleep. The doctor decided to stop the anti-psychotic medication that was clearly making me drowsy.

The discussion turned to the possibility of discharge straight from PECC instead of transferring to the general ward. I began to understand that the doctors' and nurses' intervention, along with the quiet environment within PECC, had given me an opportunity to be calm and reflective. Reaching this stage was remarkable given my extremely close encounter with suicide only eight days prior.

I welcomed the suggestion of potentially being discharged, but needed reassurance that my mood would still improve in the near future. The doctor painted a logical picture for me: I would have to continue to take the anti-depressants, as they needed more time to become fully effective in my system. This news was hard for an impatient person like me to digest. However, with my family fully aware of my illness, I felt I had the support I needed to continue my treatment.

I battled with having to wait for the medication to work for another month after being discharged, but the rewards were life changing.

Dinner was waiting for me upon my return to the common room. I consumed the roasted chicken, steamed vegetables, and a sticky date pudding with no hesitation. I never went hungry while in hospital and actually gained two kilograms.

After dinner, I watched television, spoke with the nurses and slowly increased my concentration to solve the final pieces to the jigsaw puzzle.

That evening one of the doctors notified me that my MRI and blood results had returned. Everything was normal with both tests, which left me with a very strange sense of discontent. I was frustrated with the speed of my treatment and wondered if it would have been better if one of the test results found an abnormality.

This line of thought was based on an assumption that any hypothetical illness found would have a quick fix. I hastily discounted my undesirable thoughts by reminding myself how my depression was already being successfully treated. I just needed to be patient.

PECC Day 9 – Saturday

My inability to get a full night's sleep returned immediately after I stopped taking the anti-psychotic drugs. The constant observations from the nurses throughout the night made things worse. This lack of sleep set the mood for the day – I was not in the mood to do anything.

I ate breakfast and drank two coffees to snap me out of my tiredness. I had no anticipated visits today and did not feel like repeating the unescorted leave I took yesterday. It is incredible how a bad night's sleep can influence one's whole day.

While I waited for my daily psychiatrist consultation I tried another puzzle; however, my mind wandered off to ponder my current situation.

I began to think my improved condition was directly related to how many people were helping me. Once I had asked for help, without knowing I had created a team of people to support me through my early stages of treatment.

I spent the afternoon outside in the small courtyard trying to claw back the hours of fresh air I had missed over the past week. It was during these hours in the courtyard that I made the decision to completely rid myself of the stigma associated with talking about mental illness. I planned to find a way to tell the world about my experience by opening up about depression and suicide. I started to think about how this book would come together.

After the daily routine of having my blood pressure checked I decided to have an early night. This time my sleep was aided with a sleeping tablet.

CHAPTER 8

Building my House of Cards

My consistent fixation with achieving in business manipulated all my spare time. Research and development time shifted from one year to ten years, with uninterrupted hurdles and unforeseen problems playing with my nerves. The years of trying to solve problems that kept popping up contributed to increasing stress and anxiety that was clearly spiraling out of my control.

As smartphones and computers became cheaper I quickly adopted the habit of never being disengaged from work. As soon as I finished my café job for the day, I would check emails on my phone and start working on the side business until I got home. The bus trip home was an excellent way of catching up on emails and researching ideas.

I routinely consumed my dinner in front of the computer, where the time quickly jumped from 7pm to midnight within a blink of an eye. I would take my smartphone to bed with emails bouncing around the world all night long. Before going to hospital I honestly cannot remember the last time I had a solid good night sleep.

There was no work–life balances because I could not get off the work treadmill that seemed to gather pace as the years passed by.

Work had simply taken over all aspects of every hour that I was not sleeping. There was no time put aside to zone out and explore hobbies or anything for that matter which I enjoyed doing. Do not get me wrong I was enthralled in our business venture, but it was unmistakably overwhelming my lifestyle. It had turned from a hobby into a business that I thought was too far ventured to give up now.

Unforeseen delays in the commercialization process stretched my bank balance to the limit. The majority of these hurdles resulted in unbudgeted costs, such as fighting for intellectual property rights, trial production runs, escalating IT costs, sales staff, and warehouse storage charges. The borrowings grew while the problems and delays cultivated at a faster rate. This resulted in increased stress, an inability to solve problems, and an environment that was too uncomfortable to handle.

Rays of Light

The hard work my family contributed to this business venture did result in many triumphs. When all the experts within an industry said what we wanted to achieve was not possible, there was no way I was going to give in without testing the boundaries.

About twenty production tests were performed over a period of ten years before we could produce an acceptable product. The delays between each production trial ranged from difficulties in booking in machine time for testing, to having to source new raw material suppliers, machine breakdowns, regulatory approval delays, to production plant fires, machine tooling issues, and the list went on. However, we achieved the end result that everyone in the engineering sphere said was not possible.

Obtaining intellectual property rights for our research and development was not as easy as simply lodging a patent application. We spent over six years fighting seven different patent offices around the world. Securing patents in multiple countries involved years of arguing with foreign patent offices about the semantics of certain words and phrases contained in a variety of prior art patents. The European and US patents were only granted after many appeals and court challenges. This struggle for half a decade was extremely rewarding given the hundreds of hours spent articulating our arguments.

Public acknowledgment for our dedication manifested in a variety of ways. We received recognition from international awards and in write-ups in many industry journals. The sense of achievement, moreover the satisfaction of proving others wrong was incredible, especially when the awards involved beating billion dollar companies. However, the excitement of being mentioned on TV and the USA cable channels was short lived; it did not solve the next bunch of hurdles to come our way.

A Depressive Past?

It was not until a psychiatrist provided me with literature outlining the signs and symptoms of depression that I began to evaluate my childhood and young adult years for the illness.

Upon recollection, my mood all those years ago pointed to the illness being undiagnosed for some time. I can remember feeling at least half a dozen of the symptoms during my senior school years. As I worked through my early adult years, it is now obvious some mild form of depression and anxiety was already present.

There would have been two or three moments in the past ten years where I started to retract from family and friends and generally became more withdrawn. The reason for me not responding to those situations so severely is harder to ascertain. I believe the most recent event reached the point it did because my character was tested beyond my comfort zone.

CHAPTER 9

PECC Day 10 – Sunday

Sunday was the first day where I woke up thinking that I should go home. All the medical staff had been fantastic and I was now conscious of how the past ten days presented me with a chance to start over.

After breakfast my dad and older brother came to visit. We went for a short walk to one of the hospital cafes and talked for about an hour.

The further we got into the conversation the more I became comfortable with the notion of being discharged the following week. More importantly it became easier to open up about my mood and perceptions on life. Talking to my family regarding such personal matters was previously taboo.

My family continued to layout their plans for dealing with all the problems that resulted in my breakdown. These took weeks to execute; however, just talking about the difficulties reversed some of my negative thoughts.

The daily psychiatrist consultation was brief and to the point. I would be discharged in a day or two with extensive outpatient care provided. Understanding how the hospital was going to follow up with daily phone consultations and weekly face-to-face meetings was a tremendous relief. The purpose of this extensive out-reach was to ensure I would not have a repeat episode and to monitor the effectiveness of the medication.

A very small example of how things had changed for me over the past ten days had been in my tolerance for certain things. In the past, I had hated watching reality television as I saw it as a waste of time. Now I was not fussed watching a show purely for entertain-ment.

PECC Day 11 – Monday

I was up earlier than normal on Monday. My sleep was interrupted, but this was due to the emergency helicopter landing on the roof. I only realized a cou-ple of days beforehand that the landing pad for the rescue helicopter was right next to the PECC unit.

The constant arrivals of these aircraft made me understand there were plenty of people in much more severe conditions than my own.

For as long as I can remember it was my racing

thoughts that usually caused my sleep to be interrupted. Over the past week I had observed a slowing of these thoughts, partly due to the medication, and also from the quiet environment in which I was recuperating.

After breakfast, I decided to go on another unescorted walk. I endured it for longer than the previous adventure; however, the enjoyment for fresh air and city noise had been misplaced. It now makes sense that my walking exercise over the past years was not undertaken for fitness; rather it allowed my mind the time to try to find solutions to my many overly exaggerated problems.

Within minutes of returning to PECC my mother had arrived for another impromptu visit. More importantly, she had delivered another bag full of chocolates.

The perceived stigma in talking about my illness was instantly reduced on my admission. This action now made it much easier to discuss topics like my mood and how I was feeling with my family and friends. My Mum and I discussed all matters of life and again I was rewarded with only understanding and support. Revisiting once taboo issues became simpler the more I opened up.

That afternoon I received a visit from Dad, went to my daily psychiatrist meeting, and arranged my discharge for the following day.

Dinner arrived at the usual time and the evening was spent chatting with other patients and the nurses. Before I knew it the sedative effects of the medication were taking hold, signaling that it was now time for bed.

PECC Day 12 – Tuesday

I had another bad night sleep as a result of the overnight nurse' coordinated observations. Additional noise was caused by a late night patient admission.

My mood should have been higher due to my pending discharge later that day. However, the overnight events had reduced my mood back to the around five – a clear indicator my journey to recovery was in baby steps.

An early psychiatrist consultation commenced immediately after breakfast. Two doctors, along with a trainee and a nurse attended. The nature of this meeting was indicative of my entire treatment while in the hospital. The support was incredible.

The doctors outlined the range of outpatient treatments available and the many free support programs run by various organisations, and discussed the possibility of returning to PECC if I had any inclinations my safety was at risk.

The staff's ability to address all my questions painted a very clear picture – I had made the right decision in asking for help.

On returning to the common room, two events occurred that would leave an indefinite impact on how I would move forward.

Following making my second morning coffee, the television blasted some news that was instantly shocking. My favourite actor and comedian had died. The news of Robin Williams's sudden death was more of a shock to me as soon as they reported on the cause of death: suicide.

My reaction very quickly migrated from shock to anger. I was angry because Robin Williams had removed himself from our lives. This reaction seemed very strange; I had never met him or even seen him in person, yet somehow I felt cheated.

Next, something remarkable unfolded. I immediately connected the dots. My feelings would be similar to what my family and friends would have experienced if my suicide attempt were successful.

I now understood the gravity of my illness.

My irrational actions just ten days ago could have left an indelible scar on every family member who supported me. This insidious illness can have some very confronting results.

Soon after the news of the actor's death, I received

a get-well card from my mother's sister. The card's message has stayed with me ever since; it was to signify exactly what was about to happen subsequent to my discharge:

> "It is important to remember that the beginning can be anywhere along the way." – Leigh Standley, Curly Design Inc 2013

The nurses informed me my medication had been delivered and one more medical certificate was being written as we spoke. They provided me with details about the extensive outpatient care and gave me a final piece of paperwork to fill out. I happily completed the hospital questionnaire, making very clear I was happy with the extremely high level of care I had experienced. As I finished writing the compliments, my family arrived to welcome my discharge.

My hospital stay had come to an end. Even I was overwhelmed with the difference in my persona. My mood was still anticipating a correction from the anti-depressants over a longer period; however, my asking for help twelve days ago had saved my life.

CHAPTER 10

Outpatient Care

The amazing level of support I received after simply saying those three words—"I need help"— continued beyond hospital.

I received daily phone calls from the Acute Care Team for weeks after my hospitalization. This team of doctors and nurses contacted me to monitor my mood and effects of the medication, but more importantly to ensure I was no longer experiencing suicidal thoughts.

There were times when my medication had to be altered to reflect a drop in my condition, and sleeping pills were administered to ensure my sleep patterns were brought back to normal. The Acute Care Team also arranged weekly face-to-face hourly meetings with hospital psychiatrists. These meetings answered all the questions I had, but more importantly guided me through a period where the anti-depressant medications had not fully taken effect yet.

The weeks following discharge from hospital also afforded me with twice-weekly meetings with a psychologist. I still get them mixed up with psychiatrists; but put simply, the latter can prescribe drugs. The psychologist consultations were not what I anticipated. They were informal, relaxing talks that allowed any element of my life to be explored. I had no idea that just talking to someone about the many different facets of my complicated life could be so soothing.

I spent the first couple of weeks out of hospital continuing to distance myself from stressful situations. I made sure I was nowhere near my smartphone, that I did not check emails, and that my immediate financial concerns were addressed. In addition, I completely broke free from any past daily routines that did not include eating, sleeping, and getting well.

Doctor appointments occurred about three times a week, and I had coffee and lunch with immediate family members on a daily basis. As the weeks went by I slowly re-engaged with my closest friends, but letting them know where I had been for the past month was a very difficult and touchy subject to address.

The decision to end the outpatient care, which was afforded to me by the hospital, was a joint choice. The treatment was not ended without my consultation or without my approval. After three weeks of being discharged from PECC, my mood had not lifted beyond a self-rating of five out of ten; however, my positivity had changed.

Having access to specialised mental health personnel has allowed me to better comprehend how I got myself into the situation that very nearly killed me. Being able to talk through these past events is critical for moving forward.

My treatment for this illness does not end with finishing my book. I can anticipate years of medication and months to go with professional consultations.

I see my depression as an illness that requires a constant check.

My experience was also a very abrupt way of learning that I was not living life. I was not being selfish, not providing time for me, for hobbies that would result in pleasure instead of pain. I was chasing misguided expectations generated by a naïve view of the world.

Following expert advice, I now understand my recovery will not be a straight line, I have mentally prepared myself for potential relapses by understanding how depression and anxiety manifests.

CHAPTER 11

What I Have Learnt

From my eighteen years' experience, I have five observations worth sharing. If I had a better understanding of these elements many years ago I am confident that I would have managed my symptoms or not put myself into the many situations I did.

These observations are not medical advice; rather they are pieces of information that I could have used to avoid the severity of where my life reached.

1) Anyone can ask for help.

This point is the prime reason I wrote this book.

I wanted to publish my experience for everyone to see, specifically those people who are suffering in silence and still have not had the courage to seek medical help.

My shyness stopped me from talking about my symptoms with family or friends; however, it seemed easier to ask for help from medial staff whom I did not know.

Starting from the very first day in hospital I had access to nurses, psychiatrists, psychologists, social workers, and family members. All these people were on my side; they offered their professional assistance from the moment I admitted myself into hospital. I had this incredible level of support because I put aside any stigma and said three words to the Registrar behind the desk at the emergency department: "I need help."

The decision for me to ask for help came only when I observed my own irrational actions. The very scary thought that I wish to make sure everyone fully understands is that the extent of my downward spiral could have ended my life. I was a step or two away from committing suicide. Within minutes of me trying to end my life, I acknowledged that those actions were not rational and that I needed to get help immediately.

However, even after this event I was still unable to ask family or friends for help. I had to build up courage, which took me nearly twenty-four hours, before I voluntarily admitted myself into hospital.

After experiencing the pain associated with depression, I can only recommend to those people who have not yet received treatment that they view their concerns as a potential illness—not a weakness. The treatments for depression are well researched, effective, and not cost prohibitive.

2) Understanding Your Character

During my outpatient care, I was able to start putting the pieces together with regard to how my situation came about. The most important knowledge I gained was about myself. My character held the first real clue into understanding how I reacted to those around me and to the events I faced.

Ever since I left high school, I spent the following years telling myself that hard work and dedication would yield whatever expectations I set. I then devoted over a decade trying to live up to these self-generated goals. What I failed to stop and learn so many years ago was whether my character was well matched for this journey.

I did no risk assessment to see if I was able to withstand the stresses that working long hours was placing on me.

The type of depression I was diagnosed with is called non-melancholic depression. Put simply, this means the illness is not caused by biological factors; rather it's most likely linked to stressful events I have faced. This type of depression is the most common form of the illness diagnosed.

Following my diagnosis of major depression, I undertook some research and came across invaluable information from The Blackdog Institute. This Australian-based organization identified the following distinctive personality styles that can have an influence on one's risks of developing my type of depression:

Anxious Worrying Personality Style

Someone who has an "anxious worrying" personality style tends to be highly strung, tense, nervy, and prone to stewing over things.

Irritable Personality Style

Someone who has an "irritable" personality style tends to be easily rattled and have low tolerance for frustration.

Self-critical Personality Style

A person with a "self-critical"' personality style tends to have low self-esteem and gives themself a hard time.

Rejection Sensitive Personality Style

Someone who has a "rejection sensitive" personality style tends to be hypersensitive to the quality of interpersonal relationships and perceives others as rejecting or demeaning.

Self-focused Personality Style

Someone who has a "self-focused" personality style tends to lack consideration and empathy for others, is often hostile and volatile in interacting with other people, and has a low threshold for frustration.

Perfectionistic Personality Style

A person with a "perfectionistic" personality style tends to perceive that they've failed to meet their own high standards, or that somebody has criticized their performance for being suboptimal.

Socially Avoidant Personality Style

Someone who has a "socially avoidant" personality style tends to be shy and avoids social situations for fear of their limitations being exposed or of being criticized by others.

Personally Reserved Personality Style

Finally, someone who has a "personally reserved" personality style tends to be wary of others getting too close and becomes vulnerable and depressed when their inner worlds are exposed to others.

The conclusions from their research pointed to the following:

> Those who are high on the following dimensions are at distinctly greater risk to depression (especially non-melancholic depression).
> - "Anxious Worrying" style or as a more externalized "Irritable" personality style
> - Shyness, expressed as "Social Avoidance" and/or "Personal Reserve"
> - "Self-critical"
> - "Rejection sensitive"

I view the above information about personality styles as invaluable knowledge into helping diagnose non-melancholic depression. The same institute has an online Temperament and Personality Questionnaire that I wish was available while I was at school or at university.

This questionnaire obviously has limitations, as it is a self-assessment; however, it provides an interesting summary of how personality styles can influence a person's susceptibility to non-melancholic depression. My complete results from the questionnaire are included in the Appendix; I scored high on the dimensions of Anxious Worrying, Perfectionism, Irritability, Social Avoidance, Personal Reserve,

Interpersonal Sensitivity, and Co-cooperativeness.

The importance of these results is that it identifies which personality traits I may need to modify moving forward. It is unfortunate that it took a near-death experience for me to learn how my personality styles and life events can jointly play a part in stimulating my illness. I strongly recommend you take the time to learn a little about your own personalities; the self-assessment may highlight your need to seek the aid of a healthcare professional.

3) Acknowledging a Fresh Start

Having the time to talk extensively with many different doctors about my illness resulted in several changes to my life. Overcoming the initial fear of asking for help was the beginning of this process.

My changes did not involve waking up one morning and altering every aspect of my life. After talking extensively with a psychologist, I began to make plans to change small parts of my life, one step at a time. Starting afresh was all about learning to explore what really matters.

Doctors were able to supply medical certificates that provided me with a couple of months to piece my life together. The first step forward was asking family members to oversee my finances while I was undergoing treatment. Having someone else take control of this issue allowed me to reduce the daily worries my finances were causing.

During the weeks after being discharged from hospital, I distanced myself from any work by resigning from the family business. My resignation was a vital step to ensuring my depression could be correctly treated. The decision was not difficult to make, as I knew my dedication to the business had nearly killed me. I had not given up on the project; however, it was time to start prioritizing things.

Next was getting back to basics. I resumed my good eating practices, started a course of sleeping tablets to correct my interrupted sleep, and started to talk to family and friends about my illness.

My psychologist asked me one question that I simply could not answer – what do I love doing?

After not being able to answer the question I comprehended where I was. It was time to be selfish; and as I move forward from here the decisions on what to spend my time on will be predicated on what matters – my family, my friends, and my sanity.

4) Knowing the Symptoms

I can now admit I was a master at hiding my stress and anxiety. After reading the symptoms of depression, I realized I had experienced all of them—I just did not volunteer the information to anyone. What was as equally concerning was that I did not know I had depression.

Beyond Blue lists the following symptoms—Behavior, Feelings, Thoughts, and Physical—which are associated with those that may be suffering from depression:

Behavior
- not going out anymore
- not getting things done at work/school
- withdrawing from close family and friends
- relying on alcohol and sedatives
- not doing usual enjoyable activities
- unable to concentrate

Feelings
- overwhelmed
- guilty
- irritable
- frustrated
- lacking in confidence
- unhappy
- indecisive
- disappointed
- miserable
- sad

Thoughts
- "I'm a failure."
- "It's my fault."
- "Nothing good ever happens to me."
- "I'm worthless."
- "Life's not worth living."
- "People would be better off without me."

Physical
- tired all the time
- sick and run down
- headaches and muscle pains
- churning gut
- sleep problems
- loss or change of appetite
- significant weight loss or gain

I had experienced most of these symptoms all at once, yet did nothing to remedy the situation. Before I was hospitalized, I knew my life was stressful but I simply had no understanding that I had an illness that very nearly killed me.

The reason for this illness going unchecked would be a combination of my character, ignorance, and the years of the symptoms building up.

I had reached a breaking point when I experienced practically all the symptoms at once while at the same time quitting my job and hating a career I felt stuck in.

If I had a better understanding of my own character and what the symptoms of anxiety and depression are, at the very least, I could have been aware that my symptoms were treatable if I sought help.

5) Mental Illness and the Workplace

Mental illness in the workplace deserves special mention due to the realities of the work environment. Stating that there needs to be more open discussion between employers and employees about the stigma associated with mental illness is a complex topic.

Jeopardising one's job prospects, either in securing a job or a promotion, great is of great concern for an employee with a mental health condition. Therefore, their reluctance to raise the issue of their mental health while at work is understandable.

Even when I wrote this book, it took me some time before I made the decision to publish it. I even thought about using a pen name to hide my identity, as I was conscious that any future employer may judge me based on this now public information. Obviously, it is no one's business but my own when it comes to my illness. My final choice to not hide my name when publishing this book came when I realised I would not want to work in an environment where my employer did not comprehend the need to address employee mental health issues.

There is also a sound argument for employers to address the mental health needs of their employees to minimise low productivity resulting from any long-term illness. A holistic approach in dealing with mental illness within the work environment has been addressed by The Blackdog Institute. Their factsheet titled "Workplace Wellbeing" argues for a well-rounded approach to this topic, and I strongly recommend employers and employees to read more on this issue.

Inviting work colleagues to talk to each other about their worries and mental state is all about the humility that resides within us all. My argument for raising awareness of one's mental health issues within the workplace may seem void of any reality; however, the results of not acting are not worth the risks.

Therefore, my point of view is that if employers create a more open environment for these issues to be discussed they would generate a stronger, more productive workforce.

CHAPTER 12

Time to Make Depression Topical

I am now convinced that confronting the stigma accompanying depression and suicide is where all the effort needs to be placed. Removing the stigma is a battle to be performed by those suffering the illness and everyone else in the community.

From what I have experienced since leaving hospital is that inviting people to talk about mental health issues is easier through topical discussions. Before my attempted suicide and diagnosis of major depression, I had no experience with anyone who had any mental illness. I also never thought that I would develop such an illness.

This all changed when my family and friends heard of my hospitalization and diagnosis. After talking to them, it was not long before I was informed of at least three or four people who had or still were receiving treatment for mental health issues. I was surprised by this information and it instantly put me at ease regarding talking about depression and suicide.

We tend to assume from some one's silence that they have no bubbling concerns about life's pressures. It is this silence, along with the slow and steady retraction from my social groups, which caused me so much pain. This silence needs waking up.

I have observed society's communication techniques over the past ten years eroding our social instincts. We have all been pushed into an interaction void where we use emails, texts, social media and phone calls to project our messages. Observing family and social gatherings in today's society has a common thread – everyone is in the same room but they are all glued to their mobile devices. They may be physically present but they are not engaging with the people in the room.

These technologies have made communication easier, but they have allowed us to become lazy. The level of face-to-face contact we once participated in was a natural invitation, allowing family, friends, and the work team to feel more at ease in discussing concerns.

This isolating effect breeds a poker face or blank expression. Our family members and close friends are unable to detect changes in our mood or behavior while these communication trends are intact. And what makes for a slippery slope is the time-deficient lifestyles we all lead.

I can only imagine how things would have eventuated if all my social groups made the time for face-to-face interactions. This daily invitation to talk and bounce around ideas could have led to a much softer landing when my life started to spiral out of control.

Family members need to invite each other to tell their stories and share their daily experiences. If I had made the time to spend breakfast or dinner with a family member each day, the possibility to address my many stresses over the past eighteen years would have been much higher.

The specifics of schooling curriculums and workplace training programs are thoroughly explored by The Black Dog Institute, *beyondblue*, Anxiety UK, and The Anxiety and Depression Association of America. My idea of an invitation gets back to the basic premise of looking out for those around you.

It is too lazy just to state that people with mental health concerns should break the stigma and start talking. There needs to be a concerted effort from everyone in the community to do more.

Imagine if we placed information about mental health issues on every coffee table or kitchen bench in every house in the country. Then repeated this practice in every school and workplace in every state. And what if we doubled the exposure to mental health awareness programs on television, radio, and on social media websites? The topic of depression and other mental health issues would enter the daily discourse of a much larger percentage of the population.

These daily reminders would create a talking point and would let all members of the community understand that the issue of mental illness is exactly that – an illness that has treatable practices.

EPILOGUE

I do not profess to know all the answers for battling the stigma associated with mental illness, I can only provide my opinion based on what I have experienced.

I have endured the pain of major depression to the point where my thoughts and actions became uncontrollable. My suicide attempt was brought about by a series of judgments coordinated by an irrational mind. My downward spiral brought me so close to death, so quickly, that I still find it extremely difficult to recall let alone talk about.

Yes, I have some character flaws and I worked myself way too hard; however, I learned something when I reached rock bottom—the only thing that saved me from death was asking for help.

BIBLIOGRAPHY

beyondblue , *Signs and Symptoms*, accessed 2 September 2014, http://www.beyondblue.org.au/the-facts/depression/signs-and-symptoms

Blackdog Institute, *Personality*, accessed 25 August 2014, http://www.blackdoginstitute.org.au/public/depression/causesofdepression/personality.cfm

Blackdog Institute, *Black Dog Institute Temperament and Personality questionnaire,* accessed 25 August 2014, http://www.blackdoginstitute.org.au/surveys/Temperament

Leigh Standley, The Beginning (Greeting Card), Curly Girl Designs Inc., 2013.

APPENDICES

My Black Dog Institute Temperament and Personality Questionnaire Results

'Anxious worrying':

You scored 23 on this scale. High scores (18 and over) indicate a greater tendency to become stressed, worried and anxious. If unaddressed, excessive anxious worrying can increase the risk of developing non-melancholic depression.

'Perfectionism':

You scored 31 on this scale. High scores (31 and over) are associated with a tendency to be very responsible and reliable, have high standards for oneself and to be highly committed to task and duties. While perfectionism can be a constructive characteristic, when extremely high it can actually limit one's functioning. High scorers on this dimension are somewhat less likely to get depressed than the general population. However, certain events can trigger a severe depression. These stressful events tend to involve loss of control in an important area, or the feeling that one's pride has been hurt.

'Personal reserve':

You scored 22 on this scale. High scores (17 and over) are associated with a tendency to keep one's inner feelings to oneself. People high on 'personal reserve' tend to be reluctant to let friends and acquaintances get to know them too well. Scoring high on 'personal reserve' can increase the risk of developing non-melancholic depression, particularly following events that challenge concerns about closeness.

'Irritability':

You scored 28 on this scale. High scores (21 and over) are associated with a tendency to be quick-tempered and to 'externalise' stress by becoming 'snappy' and irritated by little things. Scoring high on this dimension indicates an increased risk to brief episodes of non-melancholic depression.

'Social avoidance':

You scored 24 on this scale. High scores (17 and over) on this dimension are associated with a tendency to be introverted and to keep to oneself, while those low on this dimension tend to be very sociable.

High scores indicate a moderately increased risk to non-melancholic depression.

'Self-focused':

You scored 2 on this scale. High scores (9 and over) are associated with a tendency to prioritise one's own needs over the needs of others. People high on the 'self-focused' dimension can be more likely to develop depression when their needs are not met. However, these depressive episodes tend to be relatively brief, often because the individual externalises their frustration.

'Self-criticism':

You scored 9 on this scale. High scores (10 and over) are associated with a tendency to be quite tough on oneself. An ongoing style of self-blame and self-criticism can increase the risk of developing non-melancholic depression. However, it is important to note that most people become more self-critical when they are depressed. Thus, if you are currently depressed, a high score on this scale does not necessarily indicate an ongoing style of self-criticism.

'Interpersonal sensitivity':

You scored 14 on this scale. High scores (14 and over) are associated with a tendency to worry about rejection or abandonment. Feeling rejected in an important relationship is a common trigger for non-melancholic depression amongst people with high interpersonal sensitivity.

'Co-operativeness':

You scored 22 on this scale. High scores (20 and over) on this scale are associated with a tendency to be generally helpful, compassionate, empathic and get along well with others.

'Effectiveness':

You scored 10 on this scale. High scores (18 and over) on this scale indicate an ability to cope well with different situations and to be confident in problem-solving. People who are particularly low on the 'effectiveness' dimension may have an increased risk of developing non-melancholic depression if they encounter a stressful situation which is beyond their coping skills.

Help Lines and Key Mental Health Organizations
(Local phone numbers are listed below)

Australia

Lifeline – 13 11 14
www.lifeline.org.au

The Suicide Call Back Service – 1300 659 467
www.suicidecallbackservice.org.au

Kids Helpline – 1800 55 1800
www.kidshelp.com.au

The Black Dog Institute
www.blackdoginstitute.org.au

beyondblue
www.beyondblue.org.au

SANE Australia
www.sane.org

National Mental Health Commission
www.mentalhealthcommission.gov.au

United States of America

National Suicide Prevention Lifeline
1-800-273-8255
www.suicidepreventionlifeline.org

Trevor Project – 866-488-7386
www.thetrevorproject.org

The Anxiety and Depression Association of America
www.adaa.org

Mental Health America
www.mentalhealthamerica.net

The National Institute of Mental Health
www.nimh.nih.gov

United Kingdom

PAPYRUS – 0800 068 41 41
www.papyrus-uk.org

Samaritans – 08457 90 90 90
www.samaritans.org

Depression Alliance
www.depressionalliance.org

Anxiety UK
www.anxietyuk.org.uk

Canada

The Canadian Association for Suicide Prevention
www.suicideprevention.ca

Suicide Action Montréal
www.suicideactionmontreal.org

Kids Help Phone
www.kidshelpphone.ca

ABOUT THE AUTHOR

Anthony Bayss is a 34-year-old Sydney-based author. He recently resigned from his family business following a life-threatening bout of depression. Anthony survived an attempted suicide and bravely admitted himself into an emergency psychiatric center.

Anthony wrote *Voluntary Admission* to illustrate to everyone currently suffering an undiagnosed mental illness what events transpire once you do ask for help. The desire to tell his story was motivated by exceptional care he received while in hospital and the unwavering support since from family and friends.

CONTACT THE AUTHOR

Anthony Bayss can be contacted through the following mediums:

Website: www.voluntaryadmission.com
Email: anthonybayss@outlook.com
Twitter: @anthonybayss

Lightning Source UK Ltd.
Milton Keynes UK
UKOW04f2115220315

248284UK00002B/92/P